Mentorship Matters

Cultivating a Culture of Excellence
Through Mentorship

By Mike T. Lightner

Chief Master Sergeant (Retired), US Air Force

DARE2DREAM
LEADERSHIP DEVELOPMENT

Alaska

Printed in the United States of America

First Printing, 2024

ISBN-13:
Paperback: 979-8-9875113-3-6

Dare2Dream LD Productions
dare2dreamleadership@gmail.com

www.d2dleadership.com

TABLE OF CONTENTS

I dedicate this book to my son Tristin.

Life as a single parent hasn't been easy and I'm sure I didn't always get it right, but I am super proud of you and the Man you have become. I look forward to seeing and hearing about all the amazing things you are sure to do with your life.

I love you, Son!

Introduction

I'll never forget the first time I heard the word Mentor. As a fairly young (newly promoted) Technical Sergeant, in charge of the Aircrew Life Support section of the 90th Fighter Squadron at Elmendorf Air Force Base in Alaska. I was standing in my Commander's office and our Wing Superintendent, Master Sergeant Chris Holt, was out-briefing (this is a military term often used for providing the results of an inspection or assessment) the Commander and I on the results of a Staff Assistance Visit he had just conducted.

For those of you not familiar with the military or the term Staff Assistance Visit, it is an informal local inspection, designed to help identify and resolve small problems before they become bigger ones. At least, this is the way I tended to view them. I know others who viewed them differently, but I've always been of the mindset of "I can't fix what I don't know is broken", so I normally could see at least some value in these sorts of inspections.

However, for this particular inspection, things didn't go well, and the out-brief was a bit longer and, in my opinion, a lot more overly critical than it needed to be. It wasn't difficult to see the look of disappointment and concern on my Commander's face. I remember feeling defensive and, truth be told, embarrassed about the state of things in our shop. After all, I was the Noncommissioned Officer in Charge and everything being briefed was my responsibility.

Then it happened.

As Master Sergent Holt was concluding his out-briefing, he assured the Commander he was going to help me fix the issues and that he was "going to personally mentor me". Now, I didn't know what that meant but I didn't like the sound of that at all. The last thing I needed was someone looking over my shoulder all day, making sure I was doing things right.

Of course, I didn't say anything at the time because I really didn't even know what the word "Mentor" meant. So, my Commander and I shook Master Sergent Holt's hand, thanked him for coming and we all went our separate ways.

I remember going straight back to my office, finding the dictionary and looking up the word "Mentor" (For you young folks, before the internet became a thing, if we wanted to find the definition of a word, we had to look it up in a book called a dictionary.) and what I found, for whatever reason, kind of made me angry.

The definition read "a trusted counselor or guide." Looking back, it seems somewhat silly that I would get angry about someone wanting to be a trusted counselor or guide but at the time, I was young and apparently…not very smart…lol! In fact, my very first thought after reading this definition was "Who does he think he is? Why would I trust him? Yeah…not going to happen." And like that, the subject was closed, or so I thought.

Now, if you read my book "Lead Bold, Lead Strong, Lead Well: 9 Proven Leadership Secrets Anyone Can Learn and Apply" then you already know much of my personal story and how I came to discover and learn my passion for leadership development. If you haven't, then you may want to pick up a copy and read it. This will give you a much better understanding of what kind of an idiot I was back in those days.

Rather than repeat the entire story in this book, let's just say, over the next year or so, things in our shop didn't get any better. And the shop would stay, what myself and probably many others would call, a "hell hole", meaning everyone (including me) wanted to leave and no one wanted to come work at. That was until Master Sergeant Holt, walked into my office, sat me down and said the 17 words that changed my life.

Now as you read this, I know you're probably a bit skeptical, after all, words don't really change lives….do they? Let me tell you, we were working 12-hour days, often six days a week, and we had been doing it as long as I can remember. As the leader, I had tried everything I knew, and things were not getting any better, in fact, some were getting worse. I was tired, feeling defeated and my spirit was broken. There was a part of me that knew there had to be something else…something more…something I was missing but I didn't know what that was or where to even begin looking for it.

Although those 17 words didn't contain the answers I was looking for, now that he said them out loud, I could no longer hide from what was really going on. When he said what he said, it put the entire situation out there for the world to see and he did it in a way I could not make any more excuses.

What were the 17 words? Great question! When he said "I get the impression that you're so far underwater that you can't see the light of day." That hurt…with those words he shined a light on the root of all our problems and that root was Me. For the first time in my life, I had to admit I didn't know what I was doing. Up until now, I was able to use positional power to solve all my problems but that wasn't working and was never going to work. I knew in that moment, I needed to learn another way, and I needed to trust Master Sergeant Holt to show me. From that point on, my life would never be the same.

Mentorship has forever changed my life and it is my hope that by reading this book and applying it's principles, it will change yours and many other people's lives as well.

Chapter 1- What is Mentorship?

The dictionary definition of mentorship is: "the influence, guidance, or direction given by a mentor." Of course, this leaves a lot to be desired, so I offer the following expanded definition to be used in its place:

Mentorship is a developmental relationship in which a more experienced or knowledgeable person (the mentor) provides guidance, support, and advice to a less experienced less knowledgeable person (the mentee). The goal of mentorship is to facilitate the personal and professional growth of the mentee through shared knowledge, experiences, and perspectives.

Key elements of a positive and productive mentorship relationship include:

Guidance and Advice: The mentor offer insights, advice, and feedback based on their own experiences and expertise to help the mentee navigate their personal and professional journey.

Support and Encouragement: The mentor provides emotional support and encouragement, helping the mentee build confidence and resilience.

Skill Development: The mentor helps the mentee develop specific skills, whether technical, professional, or interpersonal, that are critical for growth and success.

Networking: The mentor often introduces the mentee to professional networks, expanding opportunities for growth, learning, and career advancement.

Goal Setting and Accountability: The mentor assists the mentee in setting big audacious goals along with realistic and achievable milestones and holds the mentee accountable for their progress.

Role Modeling: The mentor serves as a role model, exemplifying the values, behaviors, and attitudes that contribute to the mentee's success and personal fulfillment.

Knowledge Transfer: The mentor shares their knowledge, expertise, and experiences, which can help the mentee avoid common pitfalls and make informed decisions.

Mutual Learning: While the primary focus is on the mentee's development, the mentor often finds that they also learn and grow through the mentoring relationship.

In a nutshell, effective mentorship is characterized by mutual respect, trust, open communication, and a genuine commitment to the mentee's development. It can occur in various contexts, including education, the workplace, professional organizations, and personal growth/development. It can be done one-on-one or in groups. Mentorship is slow, purposeful, and targeted.

Reflect and Learn

- Which element of mentorship (e.g., guidance, support, skill development) resonates most with you, and why?

- Reflect on someone you consider a mentor—what qualities do they have that inspire you?

Chapter 2 – Responsibilities

Over the years, I've come to realize there are responsibilities that must be maintained in order for a relationship to be successful. Mentorship is no different. In fact, I've found that in a mentorship relationship, both the mentor and the mentee have distinct as-well-as shared responsibilities that contribute to the success and effectiveness of the relationship. Those responsibilities are as follows:

Shared Responsibilities

Establishing Goals and Milestones: Both the mentor and mentee should collaboratively establish big audacious goals and clear, achievable milestones for reaching them. These goals and milestones should align with the mentee's personal and professional aspirations.

Maintaining Open Communication: Both parties should ensure regular and honest communication. This involves actively listening, providing constructive feedback, and being open to discussions about progress and challenges.

Building Trust: Trust is essential for a successful mentorship relationship. Both the mentor and mentee should work to build and maintain a relationship based on mutual respect, confidentiality, and reliability.

Commitment to the Process: Both individuals must be committed to the mentorship process, dedicating time and effort to participate in meetings, discussions, and follow-up activities.

Setting Boundaries: Establishing clear boundaries regarding time, communication, and the nature of support helps maintain a healthy and productive relationship.

Mentor's Responsibilities

Providing Guidance and Feedback: The mentor should offer insights, advice, and constructive feedback based on their experience and expertise, helping the mentee navigate their career or personal development.

Role Modeling: Demonstrating professional behavior, attitudes, and values that the mentee can and should emulate. Basically, lead by example.

Sharing Knowledge and Resources: Providing access to relevant resources, tools, and networks that can support the mentee's development.

Encouraging and Motivating: Offering encouragement and motivation to help the mentee stay focused and confident in their abilities. Continually praising their specific positive choices and behaviors along the way.

Monitoring Progress: Keeping track of the mentee's progress towards their goals and milestones as well as providing positive and constructive feedback on their development.

Mentee's Responsibilities

Setting Personal Goals: The mentee should have a clear understanding of their own goals and objectives, and communicate these to the mentor.

Being Proactive: Taking initiative in the relationship by seeking advice, asking questions, and actively participating in discussions.

Being Open to Feedback: Accepting feedback and constructive criticism with an open mind, and being willing to make necessary changes or improvements.

Demonstrating Commitment: Showing dedication to personal and professional growth by following through on action plans and commitments made during mentorship meetings.

Reflecting and Acting on Advice: Reflecting on the guidance provided by the mentor and taking concrete steps to apply this advice in real-world situations.

By fulfilling these shared and individual responsibilities, both the mentor and mentee can create a productive and rewarding mentorship relationship that fosters growth, development, mutual benefit, trust, and respect.

Reflect and Learn

- How do you define success in a mentorship partnership?

- How can a mentor ensure they are leading by example?

Chapter 3 – When To Mentor

"When the student is ready, the teacher will appear."
~ Lao Tzu

When we look at ways of increasing human productivity and potential, mentorship is one of the four most commonly used tools available. The other three tools are counseling, consulting, and coaching. In order to understand which is the right tool for us to use, we must first take a brief look at each one and gain a full understanding of the problems they seek to resolve.

Counseling: A professional service provided by trained individuals (counselors or therapists) to help people address and manage personal, social, or psychological challenges. The goal of counseling is to provide a supportive environment where individuals can explore their feelings, thoughts, and behaviors, gain insights into their issues, and develop coping strategies and solutions. Counseling is the best tool for dealing with deep-seated behavioral and mental health issues and should only be done by trained and certified professionals. Generally speaking, counselors tend to be supportive and ask a lot of questions, in an effort to address situations from the past that may be causing problems in the present.

Consulting: A professional service provided by experts in a specific field who offer advice, guidance, and solutions to organizations or individuals facing specific challenges. Consultants use their specialized knowledge, skills, and experience to help clients improve performance, solve problems, and achieve their goals. These are normally short-term relationships, looking to address or assess a specific need or problem. Generally speaking, consultants tend to provide directives, instructions, or recommendations to address past or current problems.

Mentorship: As defined in a previous chapter, it is a developmental relationship in which a more experienced or knowledgeable person (the mentor) provides guidance, support, and advice to a less experienced or knowledgeable person (the mentee). The goal of mentorship is to facilitate the personal and professional growth of the mentee through shared knowledge, experiences, and perspectives. Generally speaking, mentorship tends to be more directive in nature with the mentor sharing his experiences and advice, with the expectation that the mentee will apply what he has shared. Unlike counseling and consulting, mentorship is forward looking and tends to focus on the future or solutions to existing challenges.

Coaching: A personalized, one-on-one professional development process where a trained coach works with executives, leaders, and high-potential employees to enhance their leadership skills, performance, and overall effectiveness. The goal of executive coaching is to help individuals achieve their personal and professional goals, improve their decision-making, and increase their impact within their organizations. Coaching assumes the individual has the experience and knowledge to solve the challenges they face but lack the skills or self-confidence to bring them into practice. Generally speaking, coaches tend to be supportive and ask a lot of questions. Coaching is similar to mentorship in that it is forward looking and tends to focus on the future or solutions to existing challenges.

When delivering courses on increasing human potential, I often use the following graphic to help show the difference between these for performance enhancement tools:

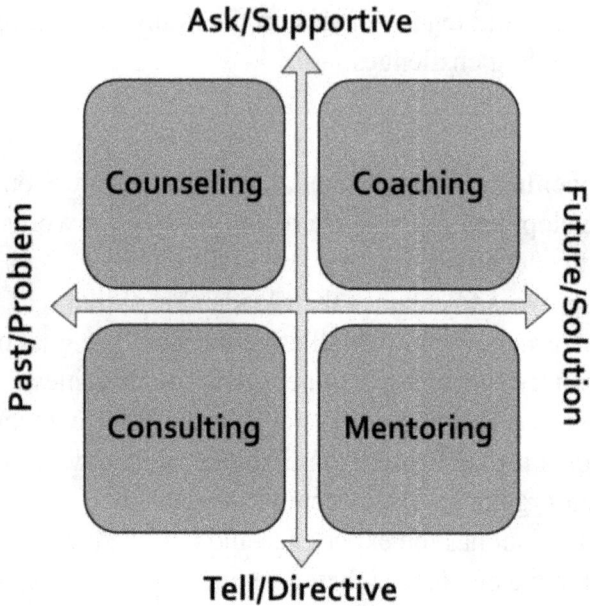

Ask/Supportive

Past/Problem

Counseling | Coaching

Consulting | Mentoring

Future/Solution

Tell/Directive

Like most things in life, if we want to fix something, we must first assess the situation and then select the correct tool. Improving human productivity and potential is no different. As you may remember from my personal story back in Chapter 1, when I first heard the word mentor, I wasn't ready. Because I wasn't ready, I resisted and pushed back.

The right time to mentor someone is when there is a clear need and/or desire by the mentee for guidance, development, or support, and when both the mentor and mentee are ready and committed to engage in a productive and meaningful relationship. Identifying the appropriate timing involves considering the individual's career stage, goals, challenges, and the availability of a compatible mentor who can provide the necessary support. As Lao Tzu would put it "When the student is ready, the teacher will appear."

It should be noted, there is no such thing as a difficult mentee. If the mentee seems difficult, it is nearly always because they are not ready to be mentored or the mentee and mentor are not a good fit for each other. In either case, the mentorship relationship simply will not work to its fullest potential and should be postponed or terminated.

Reflect and Learn

- Have you ever encountered a situation where mentorship was offered but not accepted? What happened?

- Reflect on a time when you resisted advice—what shifted your perspective to become more receptive?

Chapter 4 – Highly Effective Mentorship Process

Providing highly effective mentorship involves a structured process that ensures both the mentor and mentee gain maximum benefit from the relationship. Through many years of experience, I've found this process to be very similar for both individual and group mentorship relationships. I've also found that based on the situation, minor tweaks and adjustments will need to be made but for the most part, the following step-by-step guide will work in a large majority of cases.

Step-By-Step Guide For Mentoring Effectively:

1. Initiate the Relationship – This can be done by either the mentor or the mentee; however, as we learned from my personal example back in Chapter 1, the mentee must be ready. If the mentee is not ready, it is important that the mentor remains available and open to the possibility but not push the issue. The mentor must trust that when the mentee has reached their frustration peek, they will become receptive to outside help. Experience tells me, in many cases, the mentor will see the mentee's need long before the mentee even notices them there.

a. Identify Goals and Expectations

Clarify Objectives: Discuss and establish the mentee's goals, aspirations, and what they hope to achieve through the mentorship. I personally prefer to use the 5-year rule for setting big audacious goals. This can be hard for some people who are stuck in the moment, but I've found the earlier in the relationship you can get them to do the hard work of establishing these goals, the more productive the relationship will be.

(The 5-year rule is a simple way to help filter out the things that happen in our lives that truly matter. In simple terms, it means looking at every goal or task and deciding its impact on our life, family, relationships, team members, organization, etc. If there is no impact 5-years from now, then we shouldn't put our time or talents towards achieving that goal or accomplishing the task.)

Set Expectations: Define the roles, responsibilities, and expectations for both the mentor and mentee, including frequency and mode of communication. This is important because frustration often results in broken trust and negative feelings. I once heard a speaker say, "All frustration is a violation of expectations." and although she was talking about using the Maxwell Method of DISC to reduce conflicts in the workplace, I've found her words to be true in every relationship I have. Because of this, clearly defining roles, responsibilities, and expectations must be done before moving the relationship forward.

b. Establish Rapport – There are many people out there who will tell you rapport is built by finding commonalities between the people involved. To some extent, this is true; however, real rapport or at least the kind of rapport needed for a mentorship relationship, is established when the mentee sees the mentor has walked the path they believe they are on and has achieved the goals, status, or success the mentee desire for themselves. Things like hobbies, sports, religion, politics, etc. can be foundations for rapport but they can also lead to major blocks in the mentorship relationship, so I personally tend to stay away from them (the potential reward is just not worth the risk of losing the relationship).

Build Trust: Develop a trusting and respectful relationship by being open, honest, and approachable. Transparency is the key. Most people will learn more from hearing the mentor's mistakes then they will from hearing about their successes.

Get to Know Each Other: Spend time understanding each other's backgrounds, interests, strengths, and areas for development. One of my favorite tools to use when getting to know a mentee is the Maxwell Method of DISC (www.maxwell-disc.com). This is a powerful tool that can take a lot of the initial guess work out of the relationship. This 26-page report will give the mentor the mentee's strengths, potential weaknesses, greatest fear(s), as well as the most effective way to communicate with them as well as a host of other great information that will aid in their growth and development.

2. Plan and Set Goals

a. Create a Development Plan

Identify Areas for Growth: Assess the mentee's current skills and identify areas where they need support or development. These could start out broad in nature like: Career, Money, Health, Friends and Family, Personal Growth, Physical Environment, etc. and then get more detailed from there. For example, if I had a mentee say they wanted to become a better leader, then I would have them get a little more focused by having them pick what aspect of leadership they would like to start first. This might be something like: Communication, Results, Strategic Planning, Team Development, Decision Making, Leading Change, People Development, etc. There is power in focus and although we may eventually expand out and take on more and more of these other areas, getting them to focus in on just one, sets them up for their best chance for success.

b. Develop an Action Plan

Set SMART Milestones: Establish Specific, Measurable, Achievable, Relevant, and Time-bound milestones that the mentee can work towards their goals. The goals should be stretch goals, meaning these goals should be beyond what the mentee believes they can achieve; however, all milestones should be easily achievable steps in the direction of their goals. After completing enough of these milestones or baby-steps towards their goals, you will see the mentee's confidence and belief in their abilities grow. In fact, they may even come to realize their original stretch goal wasn't actually much of a challenge at all and adjust it to a more audacious goal.

Break Down Milestones: Outline the steps needed to achieve each milestone, including resources, training, or experiences required. Don't over complicate this. Breaking down the milestones shouldn't take longer than actually achieving them. Be specific but keep it simple.

Set Timeline: Set a timeline for key milestones to track progress and maintain momentum.

3. Engage in Regular Meetings – Mentoring is a time-consuming process and both the mentor, and the mentee must be willing to invest the time, in order for it to work. Because of this, I personally set limits on the number of people I would mentor on a one-on-one basis. For me, that number was normally around four but depending on your experience and availability, that number may be more or less. If you find you have more potential mentees than you can handle in one-on-one relationships, then group mentoring may be a better option.

a. Schedule Consistent Meetings

Regular Check-Ins: Hold regular meetings (e.g., weekly or biweekly) to discuss progress, challenges, and next steps. Consistency is the key, so it is very important that the mentor and mentee make every effort to honor their agreement and show up once the schedule has been agreed upon.

b. Foster Open Communication

Active Listening: Listen actively and empathetically to the mentee's concerns, ideas, and feedback. In my opinion, few people are taught the skills of active listening and others who have the skills are often in to much of a hurry to actually use them. Here are some common steps for active listening:

- Be Present: Clear your mind of distractions and focus entirely on the speaker.

- Use Positive Body Language: Show that you are engaged with non-verbal cues such as nodding and appropriate facial expressions.

- Practice Patience: Allow the speaker to express their thoughts fully before responding.

- Ask Open-Ended Questions: Encourage deeper conversation by asking questions that cannot be answered with a simple "yes" or "no."

- Reflect and Summarize: Regularly reflect back what you've heard and summarize key points to ensure understanding.

Provide Constructive Feedback: Offer honest, specific, and actionable feedback to help the mentee improve and grow. I've found that using the sandwich technique very helpful when providing feedback. What this means is that feedback is provided in a layered approach. First some positive feedback, then some potentially negative/constructive feedback, followed quickly by some more positive and encouraging feedback. For most people, this will make the feedback a little easier to accept and take corrective action.

4. Support and Challenge the Mentee

a. Offer Guidance and Resources – This is really the heart of the mentorship relationship.

Share Knowledge and Experience: Provide insights, advice, and lessons learned from your own experiences. This is where the mentor will bring all of their knowledge, skills and experience into play. In many cases, the world the mentor gained their knowledge, skills, and experience in, no longer exists. Because of this, the mentor must be able to take what they hear/learn and apply it in new and innovative ways in order to meet their unique challenges. Mentors must remain open to this reality and not maintain the expectation that the mentee will do things exactly like the mentor had done them in the past.

Recommend Resources: Suggest relevant books, articles, courses, and other resources that can aid the mentee's development. We live in a world where there are more free learning resources available than any other time in history. It is appropriate and in many cases necessary for the mentor to help guide the mentee to the resources they believe will help the mentee the most. It is also appropriate for the mentor to assign some of these resources as study work, to be viewed or read by the mentee before the next meeting and then discussed. I've even found it useful to use some of these resources during the mentorship meeting to help create talking points or provide additional context in the area of most interest to the mentee. In fact, this works extremely well in a group mentorship environment. Bottom line, be creative, see what works best for you and your mentee and adjust as necessary.

b. Encourage Critical Thinking and Problem-Solving

Ask Open-Ended Questions: Encourage the mentee to think critically and explore different perspectives. Early on in the mentorship relationship, the mentor may find themselves dominating much of the conversation; however, over time this should flip to a more coaching or questioning type of relationship. For this natural and necessary progression to take place, the mentor must understand and use good open-ended questioning.

Here are some examples of what those might look like:

- General Inquiry:

"Can you tell me more about your experience with...?"

"What are your thoughts on the current situation?"

"How do you feel about the changes happening in…?"

- Personal Growth and Development:

"What are some of your long-term career goals?"

"How have your past experiences shaped who you are today?"

"What skills would you like to develop further, and why?"

- Problem-Solving and Decision-Making

"What are some potential solutions you can think of for this issue?"

"How do you approach making difficult decisions?"

"What factors do you consider most important when solving a problem?"

- Feedback and Reflection

"What do you think went well during the project, and what could have been improved?"

"How did you feel about your performance in the last quarter?"

"What feedback have you received that has been most helpful to you?"

- Team Dynamics and Collaboration

"How do you prefer to work within a team?"

"What are some ways we can improve our team's collaboration?"

"Can you describe a time when you successfully resolved a conflict with a colleague?"

- Leadership and Management

"What qualities do you think are most important for a good leader?"

"How do you motivate and inspire your team?"

"What leadership challenges have you faced, and how did you overcome them?"

- Innovation and Creativity

"How do you come up with new ideas and innovations?"

"What inspires you to think creatively?"

"Can you share an example of a creative solution you implemented?"

Tips For Using Open-Ended Questions Effectively:

- Be Genuine: Show genuine interest in the responses by actively listening and engaging in the conversation.

- Follow Up: Use follow-up questions to delve deeper into the initial responses (e.g., "Can you explain more about that?" or "What led you to that conclusion?").

- Create a Safe Environment: Ensure that the person feels comfortable and respected, which encourages them to share more openly.

- Avoid Leading Questions: Ensure your questions are neutral and do not suggest a particular answer or direction.

Support Independence: Empower the mentee to make their own decisions and take ownership of their development. Anyone who has ever experienced professional or executive coach knows, people who come up with their own solutions are much more likely to follow through with their own solutions. This holds true for mentorship as well. The goal of any personal or professional development program should always be to get the individual, in this case the mentee, to the point where they can out grow the person helping them. To take what they are learning and elevate it to the next level. This can only happen, if the person being helped is taught how to think rather than what to think.

5. Monitor Progress and Provide Feedback

a. Track Progress – From my experience, this is best done by the mentee. Although it may be necessary for the mentor to keep some notes related to the meeting in order to provide proper follow-up, the bulk of the responsibilities for tracking progress should be the responsibility of the mentee. This seems to help keep them more engaged with the meetings and puts the ownership in the hands of the person who stands to gain the most from the relationship.

Review Milestones and Goals Regularly: Revisit the mentee's milestones, goals, and action plan periodically to assess progress and make adjustments as needed. Normally, what seems to work best is for the mentee develop and agree to complete a or some milestone(s) at the end of each meeting. The first thing discussed at the next meeting would be their progress in achieving the milestone(s) and/or what they had learned along the way. Then, once a quarter, do a full review of all the progress made, the lessons learned and how these fit into the ultimate goal(s). Doing this, allows for necessary adjustments to be made to the milestones, goals and action plan in a timely and more effective manner.

Celebrate Achievements: Acknowledge and celebrate milestones and successes to motivate the mentee. This is a critical part to the mentorship process and must not be overlooked. Celebrating the wins helps to build the momentum that will be needed to push through the next challenge. The celebration should be in line with the mentee's wishes and something they feel is appropriate and exciting. I've found it particularly helpful to ask them early on in the relationship how they would like to celebrate their wins. This takes much of the guess work out of it and can keep the mentor from over or under doing it.

b. Provide Ongoing Feedback – As discussed in step 3b, feedback is an important part of the communication part of this relationship. It must be both timely and balanced to be most effective.

Timely Feedback: Provide feedback in a timely manner to address issues and reinforce positive behaviors.

Balanced Feedback: Offer a mix of positive reinforcement and constructive criticism to support balanced growth.

6. Conclude the Mentorship Relationship – Begin with the end in mind is a statement that has permeated the business sector for many years and mentorship is no different. As the mentee grows and develops, there will come a time where they have learned all they can from one mentor and must move onto another. This is a necessary and nature part of the growth process and understanding this upfront can help when it is time to transition when the time comes.

It should be noted, that at any time during the mentorship relationship, if the mentor senses there may be a situation or conflict of interest which may prevent them from continuing, they must end the mentorship relationship immediately. For example, if a male mentor starts to gain personal feelings towards a female mentee which may result in an inappropriate personal or sexual relationship. Because the mentor's position gives them informal power over the mentee, it is the mentor's responsibility to acknowledge the change in circumstance and end the mentorship relationship.

a. Plan for Transition

Prepare for Closure: Discuss the conclusion of the formal mentoring relationship and plan for a smooth transition. As the mentor sees the mentee growing to the edge of their ability to prograde help, they must start the transition process. This can be done by simply ending the mentorship relations or the mentor can assist the mentee in helping them find someone who can take over where they left off. In either case, the mentor must be ready to take the appropriate steps when necessary.

Summarize Achievements: Review the mentee's progress and achievements over the course of the mentorship. This is a great opportunity to celebrate all the wins and encourage them to continue their growth and development.

b. Maintain the Connection

Future Contact: Agree on how you will stay in touch and continue to support each other informally. Just because the mentorship relationship has ended, doesn't mean the relationship itself must come to an end. On the contrary, I've found that these relationships can evolve into long term friendships. In fact, to this day, even though I've long since retired, I still maintain contact with several people who once mentored me and dozens of people who I once mentored.

Network Inclusion: Introduce the mentee to your professional network to help them continue their growth and development. One of my favorite things to do at the end of a mentorship relationship, was to match my mentee with a potential new mentor. Often times, if I knew a mentorship relationship was coming to an end, I would schedule a lunch with my mentee and someone who I thought would be a good next mentor for them. Then, at lunch I would help facilitate the conversation and encourage the two of them to get together for a one-on-one conversation.

By following these steps, mentors can provide highly effective mentorship that supports the mentee's personal and professional growth, builds a strong and trusting relationship, and ensures meaningful and lasting outcomes. When done right, mentorship helps both parties grow and develop and can even lead to long term friendships.

Reflect and Learn

- Why is it essential to establish a timeline for milestones, and how can this maintain momentum?

- Reflect on a time when constructive feedback helped you grow—what made it impactful?

Chapter 5 – Cultivating a Culture of Followership

If you have read this far, you must have realized by now that mentorship is a powerful tool that can help individuals develop their skills, knowledge, and confidence in a particular field. One aspect of mentorship that is often overlooked is the impact it can have on followership. Followership is the ability to effectively follow and support a leader, and it is an essential skill in any organization. A culture of followership is one where individuals are empowered to support their leaders, contribute to the success of the organization, and take ownership of their roles and responsibilities. The US Air Force is a great example of an organization that cultivates a culture of mentorship and in doing so, fully capitalized on the power of enthusiastically committed followership.

By cultivating a culture of mentorship, organizations can empower their employees to become better followers, leading to increased collaboration, communication, and productivity. As you have undoubtebly discovered by now, one of the key benefits of mentorship is the development of trust between mentors and mentees. Trust is essential for effective followership, as followers must trust their leaders to make decisions that are in the best interest of the organization and its people.

By building trust through mentorship, mentees can learn to trust their leaders and follow their guidance with confidence.

Mentorship also helps to develop communication skills, which are essential for effective followership and future growth into leadership roles within the organization. Mentors can provide feedback and guidance on how to communicate effectively with leaders, colleagues, and clients. By developing strong communication skills, mentees can better understand their roles and responsibilities within the organization, significantly increasing their contribution to its success.

Another benefit (in my opinion, one of the biggest benefits) of mentorship is the development of critical thinking skills. Mentors will challenge mentees to think critically about their work, their goals, and their role within the organization. By developing critical thinking skills, mentees can become more independent and proactive followers, taking ownership of their responsibilities, and contributing innovative ideas to the organization.

Mentorship also helps to build resilience in followers. By providing support and guidance, mentors can help mentees navigate challenges and setbacks in their careers. Resilient followers are able to bounce back from failures, adapt to change, and continue to support their leaders and colleagues in achieving their individual and organizational goals.

Along with resiliency, mentorship can also help to develop emotional intelligence in followers. Emotional intelligence is the ability to understand and manage one's own emotions, as well as the emotions of others. By developing emotional intelligence through mentorship, followers can better navigate interpersonal relationships, resolve conflicts, and collaborate effectively with their colleagues.

To cultivate a culture of followership through mentorship, organizations can implement mentorship programs that provide opportunities for employees to develop relationships with mentors who can support their personal and professional growth. These programs can be formal, with structured mentorship relationships and goals, or informal, with mentors and mentees connecting organically within the organization.

It should be noted; formal organizational mentorship programs that assign mentors to mentees (forced matching), like they are issuing them a tool or piece of equipment, rarely work and should be avoided. Instead, organizations should encourage leaders at all levels to cultivate professional relationships with the people in the organization and seek out those who are ready and would benefit from being mentored by them.

Another trend I've seen pop up recently is the idea of "speed mentoring" which in my opinion is ridiculous and potentially more damaging to the organization than forced matching.

I am absolutely fundamentally against "speed mentoring" and everything that it represents. This is based on my belief of what a mentor is and how mislabeling an event like this, tarnishes the word and everything it represents.

In fact, I received an email once asking me to be part of a "speed mentoring" panel for an event hosted by an organization here in Anchorage, Alaska. Anyone who has ever worked with me in the military or read any of my books knows that I have strong feelings and beliefs associated with mentorship. They will also know what being mentored has done for me in my career and life.

With this in mind, I share with you my response to their request:

Thank you for the invitation; however, I must decline.

As much as I appreciate the work your organization does with kids, I do not believe in the principle or philosophy of "Speed Mentoring." In fact, over my 30 plus years of experience in leadership and the development of human potential, I have found true life changing mentorship to be anything but "speedy." You see, I believe mentorship is as much about the relationship as it is about the exchange of information. Anyone can provide advice based on their experience but being a mentor is about so much more...it's about changing behavior in a way that positively transforms lives. This simply can't be done in an 8-minute one-off meeting. There is no microwaving mentorship, it must be put in the slow cooker and allowed to simmer for as long as needed for the transformation to take place.

I believe when we mislabel events like this, when we misuse the word mentoring, we misrepresent what a mentor is and the positive impact one can have in someone's life. Worse yet, we teach people (in this case our young impressionable kids) that being mentored is easy, fun and quick. Then, when a real mentorship relationship presents itself, they reject it because it's hard, messy and time consuming. The words we use matter and how we use them matters even more.

Again, I love what it is that your organization is trying to do for our kids, I just can't with any integrity help out with this project.

I hope you understand,

Mike

Sadly, the organization hosting this event never responded. Part of me wishes they had because I had some great ideas on how to help them transform their current idea into one that could develop a long-term mentorship program.

One example went something like this: Using this event as a launchpad and relabeling it as "mentorship matchup", this event would give an opportunity for mentees to connect with potential mentors and vice versa. At the event, each mentee would meet with each of the mentors for an 8-minute one-on-one. If, during this initial short meeting, they both agreed to move forward with a more formal mentorship relationship, they could exchange contact information and set a date and time for a follow-up meeting. However, each mentee would be limited to only one mentor and each mentor could only accept three mentees. Anyways, that was the idea.

Another way organizations can help cultivate a culture of mentorship is by providing training and resources to mentors and mentees to help them develop the skills and knowledge necessary for effective mentorship. This can include workshops on communication, emotional intelligence, and leadership, as well as resources such as books, articles, and online courses on mentorship and followership.

By investing in mentorship programs and developing a culture of mentorship within their organizations, leaders can empower their employees to become better followers, contributing to the success of the organization and fostering a collaborative and supportive work environment. Organizations that invest in mentorship programs and develop a culture of mentorship will see increased collaboration, communication, and productivity, leading to greater success and satisfaction among their employees.

Reflect and Learn

- What role does mentorship play in developing critical thinking among followers?

- Reflect on a situation where mentorship improved your ability to collaborate—what lessons did you learn?

Chapter 6 – Mentorship Do's and Don'ts

From my experience, by adhering to these do's and don'ts, mentors can create a supportive, productive, and effective mentoring relationship that fosters growth and development for their mentees.

Mentor Do's

Do Establish Clear Goals: Set specific, measurable, and achievable goals for the mentorship relationship.

Do Listen Actively: Pay full attention to the mentee's concerns, ideas, and feedback.

Do Provide Constructive Feedback: Offer honest, actionable, and supportive feedback.

Do Be Open-Minded: Be receptive to new ideas and perspectives.

Do Be Patient: Understand that growth and learning take time.

Do Encourage Questions: Foster a safe environment where asking questions is encouraged.

Do Share Your Experiences: Offer insights from your own experiences, including successes and failures.

Do Respect Confidentiality: Keep shared information private and confidential.

Do Set Regular Meetings: Schedule consistent check-ins to maintain momentum and accountability.

Do Celebrate Achievements: Acknowledge and celebrate the mentee's accomplishments.

Do Be Empathetic: Show understanding and compassion towards the mentee's challenges.

Do Provide Resources: Share relevant articles, books, and other resources.

Do Be a Role Model: Demonstrate the behaviors and values you advocate.

Do Adapt Your Approach: Tailor your mentoring style to fit the mentee's needs.

Do Foster Independence: Encourage the mentee to make their own decisions and think critically.

Do Set Boundaries: Define the limits of the mentoring relationship to maintain professionalism.

Do Be Honest: Provide truthful insights and advice, even when it's difficult.

Do Focus on Development: Emphasize personal and professional growth over quick fixes.

Do Encourage Networking: Help the mentee build their professional network.

Do Follow Up: Check in on the mentee's progress and challenges regularly.

Mentor Don'ts

Don't Dominate the Conversation: Allow the mentee to speak and express themselves.

Don't Be Judgmental: Avoid criticizing or making the mentee feel inadequate.

Don't Micromanage: Give the mentee space to grow and make their own decisions.

Don't Overpromise: Be realistic about what you can offer and deliver.

Don't Be Disinterested: Show genuine interest and enthusiasm in the mentee's development.

Don't Avoid Difficult Topics: Address challenging issues openly and constructively.

Don't Impose Your Views: Respect the mentee's values and perspectives.

Don't Rush the Process: Allow time for the mentee to reflect and implement changes.

Don't Ignore Boundaries: Respect the professional limits of the relationship.

Don't Provide All the Answers: Encourage the mentee to find solutions independently.

Don't Criticize Publicly: Offer feedback in private, not in front of others.

Don't Neglect the Relationship: Stay committed and actively involved in the mentorship.

Don't Be Inconsistent: Maintain regular communication and meetings.

Don't Focus Solely on Weaknesses: Recognize and build on the mentee's strengths.

Don't Be Vague: Provide clear, specific, and actionable advice.

Don't Dismiss Small Achievements: Acknowledge all progress, big or small.

Don't Be Unapproachable: Foster an open and approachable demeanor.

Don't Interrupt: Allow the mentee to finish their thoughts before responding.

Don't Be Overly Critical: Balance feedback with positive reinforcement.

Don't Assume Understanding: Ensure the mentee comprehends your advice and guidance.

Although similar to the mentor's list of Do's and Don'ts, the mentees list is slightly different, so I thought it was worth providing it separately. By following these do's and don'ts, mentees can ensure a productive and beneficial mentorship relationship that fosters personal and professional growth.

Mentee Do's

Do Be Proactive: Take the initiative to schedule meetings and follow up.

Do Set Clear Goals: Define what you hope to achieve from the mentorship.

Do Listen Actively: Pay full attention to your mentor's advice and feedback.

Do Show Appreciation: Express gratitude for your mentor's time and guidance.

Do Be Open to Feedback: Accept constructive criticism and use it to improve.

Do Prepare for Meetings: Come to meetings with specific questions or topics to discuss.

Do Be Honest: Share your true thoughts, concerns, and aspirations.

Do Follow Through: Act on the advice and tasks agreed upon with your mentor.

Do Reflect on Advice: Take time to consider how your mentor's guidance applies to your situation.

Do Be Respectful of Time: Be punctual and considerate of your mentor's schedule.

Do Keep an Open Mind: Be willing to explore new ideas and perspectives.

Do Seek Clarification: If you don't understand something, ask for clarification.

Do Set Boundaries: Establish professional boundaries to maintain a healthy relationship.

Do Track Progress: Keep a record of your progress and accomplishments.

Do Be Enthusiastic: Show enthusiasm and commitment to your personal growth.

Do Be Reliable: Follow through on commitments and show consistency.

Do Communicate Regularly: Keep in touch with your mentor and provide updates on your progress.

Do Self-Reflect: Regularly assess your own performance and growth.

Do Be Patient: Understand that growth takes time and effort.

Do Network: Use your mentor's guidance to build your professional network.

Mentee Don'ts

Don't Be Passive: Avoid relying solely on your mentor to drive the relationship.

MENTORSHIP MATTERS

Don't Take Criticism Personally: View feedback as an opportunity for growth.

Don't Be Afraid to Ask Questions: Clarify any doubts or uncertainties you have.

Don't Ignore Advice: Take your mentor's advice seriously and consider its application.

Don't Be Disrespectful: Always be polite and considerate in your interactions.

Don't Cancel Last Minute: Avoid cancelling meetings at the last minute unless absolutely necessary.

Don't Expect Immediate Results: Understand that personal and professional growth takes time.

Don't Be Defensive: Accept feedback without becoming defensive or dismissive.

Don't Overburden Your Mentor: Be mindful of the time and effort your mentor is investing.

Don't Ignore Professional Boundaries: Maintain a professional relationship with your mentor.

Don't Assume: Don't make assumptions about your mentor's advice or intentions; seek clarification.

Don't Be Dishonest: Always be truthful about your progress and challenges.

Don't Neglect Preparation: Always come prepared for meetings with your mentor.

Don't Be Impatient: Understand that significant progress may take time to manifest.

Don't Expect All Answers: Be prepared to seek solutions independently as well.

Don't Be Unapproachable: Maintain a positive and approachable demeanor.

Don't Neglect Your Responsibilities: Fulfill your own duties and tasks diligently.

Don't Blame Others: Take responsibility for your actions and learn from mistakes.

Don't Be Overly Critical of Yourself: Accept that making mistakes is part of the learning process.

Don't Forget to Self-Care: Maintain a healthy balance between mentorship activities and personal well-being.

By following these do's and don'ts, mentees can ensure a productive and beneficial mentorship relationship that fosters personal and professional growth.

Chapter 7 – Group Mentorship

After completing this book and sending it off to my editor for their initial review, I realized I was missing something. Then it came to me in a flash, I had forgotten to share my thoughts and experience on group mentoring. As I reviewed all the previous chapters, looking for a place to plug it in, I realized that group mentoring was more of an advanced skillset. Because of this, it should only be done by more advanced mentors. This gave me two options, one leave it out or two add it in as a stand-alone chapter.

Group Mentorship has had too much of an impact on my life and business to simply leave it out, so over the next few pages, I'll do my best to share my experience and thoughts on the subject.

My Introduction to Group Mentoring

Shortly after joining the John Maxwell Team (now call Maxwell Leadership) in 2013, I joined their Mentorship program. In this program, they used a group mentorship call in format where there could be a few or hundreds of people on a single call. This was my first experience with group mentoring and I'll admit, at first, it was a bit intimidating.

Over the years that followed, as my business became busier, I simply hadn't made the time to get on many Mentorship calls. However, a few years in, I felt stuck, business was ok but only because I was working really really hard to sell people into my events. As much as I loved hosting events and changing people's lives, I knew there was something I was missing...there had to be an easier way to turn my dream and passion into a profitable business, with less effort.

One day, I had an open block of time on my schedule that lined up with one of the Mentor's (Paul Martinelli) calls, so I jumped on the line. I didn't have a question, but I just felt like if I listened in...if I just opened my mind to the questions of other, more experienced people, and leaned into Paul's answers, something would present itself...something would speak to me.

I honestly don't remember who was on the call or any of the questions that were asked but I do remember at one point Paul said "how do I spend $10,000 with you?" he then said something like "if I were to walk into your business today with a check for $10,000, do you have a program you could sell me?"

As soon as I heard this, I knew…I don't know how…but I just knew this is what I needed to hear. So, I jumped off the line and started thinking through what a $10,000 leadership and personal development program would look like. Then I started taking different John Maxwell Team resources and packaging them together into a modular program that I could customize and use for presentations and workshops anywhere from 10 minutes to 3 days long.

A few weeks later, someone from the nearby Air Force base called me and asked me if I could come in and give them some advice on how to build a weeklong training program for their people. Of course I said yes and went. Toward the end of the meeting, I could see their content goal and launch timeline were not lining up. Clearly, the Commander could see this as well and looked at me and said "Mr. Lightner, you see what we are up against, what can you do to help?" I looked him in the eye, pointed towards the board and said with a confidence that surprised even me, "I can take all of that, it will take 3 days and will cost you $10,000." He looked around the room, looked back and me and said "Done!"

Over the next 9 months or so, I used the building blocks of that program to secure two more similar contracts. The best part is, I didn't have to secure a venue, audio/visual equipment, worry about food/refreshments or even sell a single ticket, the organizations were doing all that for me. Through Group Mentoring, I was able to get the answer to a question I wasn't experienced enough to know I should be asking.

From this experience and many others that followed, I've learned there are three key advantages to Group Mentoring:

1. Diverse Perspectives and Collective Wisdom

Group mentorship brings together a variety of individuals, each with unique experiences, skills, and insights. This diversity allows mentees to gain a broader range of perspectives and solutions to challenges by hearing the answers to questions they may not even have known they should have been asking. The collective wisdom of the group fosters creative problem-solving and innovative thinking, as mentees benefit from the shared knowledge and experiences of the mentor as-well-as their peers.

2. Enhanced Support and Networking

In a group mentorship setting, mentees have the opportunity to connect not only with their mentor but also with each other. This creates a supportive community where individuals can share their experiences, offer encouragement, and build a network of like-minded peers. The relationships formed in group mentorship can lead to lasting professional connections and collaborative opportunities, broadening the mentees' access to resources and support.

3. Accelerated Learning and Development

Group mentorship accelerates learning by exposing mentees to a variety of real-world scenarios, challenges, and solutions in a condensed timeframe. The interactive nature of group discussions, role-playing, and collaborative exercises allows mentees to practice new skills and receive immediate feedback from both the mentor and their peers. This dynamic environment promotes rapid personal and professional growth, as mentees can quickly apply what they've learned in a safe, supportive setting.

The process for group mentoring is basically the same as one-on-one mentoring, however, the mentor must be sure to maintain control of the environment to ensure each person is getting their question(s) answered in a supportive and productive way. This isn't a forum for other mentees to try to look good by answering other mentees questions or grandstand with long detailed stories before asking their question. The mentees must come prepared with a well thought out and crafted question and trust the mentor to ask for additional context if they believe it is needed to properly answer the question.

This is one of the reasons doing group mentorship over a phone service like https://www.freeconferencing.com/ is so effective. Because it gives the mentor the ability to mute everyone's line and only open one line at a time when it is time to answer questions.

Choosing individual or group mentorship can be based on a variety of different factors. Things like availability of the mentor, price, proximity, etc… are all things to think about. However, regardless of what form of mentorship you choose, it is clear that everyone can benefit from mentorship. So, if you don't currently have a mentor or offer mentorship to the people around you, I'd recommend you start looking for opportunities right away.

Reflect and Learn

- What are the potential advantages of diverse perspectives in group mentorship settings?

-..Reflect on a time when you learned from someone else's question—how might this apply to group mentorship?

Reflect and Learn

- What role does peer interaction play in the success of group mentorship programs?

- How can group mentorship provide networking opportunities for participants?

Chapter 8 – Additional Resources

Thank you for investing in yourself and learning about mentorship. As you could probably tell, this is a subject that I am very passionate about and I hope this book helped to spark or further add to your passion as well. I would encourage you to not stop here. Continue to study this subject and learn what you can from other thought leaders as-well. The following list of books covers various aspects of mentorship, from practical guides and strategies to personal stories and theoretical frameworks, providing valuable insights for both mentors and mentees. I hope you will check some of them out and that they will help you on your growth journey.

"Mentoring 101: What Every Leader Needs to Know" by John C. Maxwell

"The Mentor Leader: Secrets to Building People and Teams That Win Consistently" by Tony Dungy

"Dare to Lead: Brave Work. Tough Conversations. Whole Hearts." by Brené Brown

"One Minute Mentoring: How to Find and Work With a Mentor – and Why You'll Benefit from Being One" by Ken Blanchard and Claire Diaz-Ortiz

"Everyone Needs a Mentor" by David Clutterbuck

"Power Mentoring: How Successful Mentors and Proteges Get the Most Out of Their Relationships" by Ellen A. Ensher and Susan E. Murphy

"The Heart of Mentoring: Ten Proven Principles for Developing People to Their Fullest Potential" by David A. Stoddard with Robert J. Tamasy

"Managers as Mentors: Building Partnerships for Learning" by Chip R. Bell and Marshall Goldsmith

"The Mentoring Manual: Your Step-by-Step Guide to Being a Better Mentor" by Julie Starr

"Mentorship: A Path to Success" by Jill A. Brown and Annette N. Shelley

"Starting Strong: A Mentoring Fable" by Lois J. Zachary and Lory A. Fischler

"You Win in the Locker Room First: The 7 C's to Build a Winning Team in Business, Sports, and Life" by Jon Gordon and Mike Smith (emphasizes mentorship in leadership).

Chapter 9 – Mentorship Success Shorts

There is seemingly no end to the list of people who credit mentorship for their success (including me). However, to help drive home the power of mentorship, I felt it fitting to provide you with just a few examples of people you may recognize along with what they believed mentorship did for them.

1. Howard Schultz

Who They Are: Former CEO of Starbucks.

How Mentorship Helped: Howard Schultz was mentored by the original Starbucks founders, who taught him about the importance of creating a community-focused brand. They provided him with insights into the coffee business and customer experience, helping Schultz transform Starbucks into a global brand.

Better Followers: Schultz learned to value the wisdom and experience of others, making him a more collaborative and open-minded leader.

Passing It On: Schultz mentored many executives within Starbucks, emphasizing ethical leadership and customer focus. He also wrote books sharing his leadership philosophies and experiences.

2. Oprah Winfrey

Who They Are: Media mogul and former talk show host.

How Mentorship Helped: Oprah was mentored by Maya Angelou, who provided her with wisdom, confidence, and a deeper understanding of herself and her potential. This mentorship was crucial in Oprah's personal and professional development.

Better Followers: Oprah learned the importance of empathy, humility, and continuous learning, making her more receptive to feedback and diverse perspectives.

Passing It On: Oprah mentored numerous individuals, including Dr. Phil McGraw, helping them build successful careers. She also established the Oprah Winfrey Leadership Academy for Girls in South Africa, emphasizing education and empowerment.

3. Sheryl Sandberg

Who They Are: COO of Facebook and author of "Lean In."

How Mentorship Helped: Sheryl was mentored by Larry Summers, who guided her career moves and encouraged her to take risks and assert herself. This mentorship played a significant role in her professional success and confidence as a leader.

Better Followers: Sandberg learned to appreciate constructive feedback and the importance of diverse viewpoints, enhancing her ability to lead collaboratively.

Passing It On: Sandberg mentors many women in tech and business, advocating for gender equality in the workplace. Her Lean In organization supports women through mentorship and community building.

4. Elon Musk

Who They Are: CEO of SpaceX and Tesla.

How Mentorship Helped: Elon Musk was mentored by Jim Cantrell, an aerospace engineer, who provided technical knowledge and strategic advice crucial for the early stages of SpaceX. Cantrell's mentorship helped Musk navigate the complex aerospace industry.

Better Followers: Musk learned to value expert advice and to surround himself with knowledgeable individuals, making him more effective in seeking and applying insights from his team.

Passing It On: Musk mentors young engineers and entrepreneurs, encouraging innovation and resilience. He frequently shares his experiences and advice on tackling challenges and pursuing ambitious goals.

5. Indra Nooyi

Who They Are: Former CEO and Chairperson of PepsiCo.

How Mentorship Helped: Nooyi was mentored by Roger Enrico, the former CEO of PepsiCo. Enrico guided her in strategic thinking and leadership skills, helping her navigate complex business challenges and develop a visionary approach to leadership.

Better Followers: Nooyi's mentorship experience taught her the importance of listening, learning from others, and valuing diverse perspectives.

Passing It On: Nooyi mentored many emerging leaders within and outside PepsiCo, emphasizing strategic vision, work-life balance, and fostering supportive work environments.

6. Serena Williams

Who They Are: Professional tennis player.

How Mentorship Helped: Serena was mentored by her father, Richard Williams, who coached her from a young age, instilling resilience, strategic thinking, and a champion's mindset.

Better Followers: Williams learned the importance of discipline, dedication, and listening to her coach's insights, which she applied throughout her career.

Passing It On: Serena mentors young athletes, sharing her experiences and the lessons she learned from her father. She also advocates for women's rights and equality in sports, inspiring the next generation to pursue their dreams.

7. Mark Zuckerberg

Who They Are: CEO of Facebook.

How Mentorship Helped: Mark Zuckerberg was mentored by Steve Jobs, who provided invaluable advice on management, product focus, and maintaining a mission-driven company culture.

Better Followers: Zuckerberg learned the value of seeking guidance and feedback from experienced leaders, making him more receptive to insights from his team.

Passing It On: Zuckerberg mentors other tech entrepreneurs, sharing his experiences and fostering a culture of innovation. He has supported many startups through initiatives like Internet.org.

8. Eric Schmidt

Who They Are: Former CEO of Google.

How Mentorship Helped: Schmidt was mentored by John Doerr, a venture capitalist, who provided strategic guidance and support as Google scaled rapidly. Doerr's mentorship helped Schmidt navigate the challenges of leading a high-growth company.

Better Followers: Schmidt learned the importance of seeking external perspectives and integrating diverse viewpoints into strategic decisions.

Passing It On: Schmidt has mentored numerous tech leaders and executives, emphasizing the importance of strategic thinking and innovation. He co-authored books sharing his leadership insights.

9. Malala Yousafzai

Who They Are: Pakistani education activist and Nobel laureate.

How Mentorship Helped: Malala was mentored by her father, Ziauddin Yousafzai, who encouraged her to speak out for girls' education and provided unwavering support.

Better Followers: Malala learned the importance of advocacy, resilience, and listening to diverse voices, enhancing her ability to lead effectively.

Passing It On: Malala founded the Malala Fund to support education initiatives globally. She mentors young girls, encouraging them to pursue education and leadership roles.

10. Richard Branson

Who They Are: Founder of the Virgin Group.

How Mentorship Helped: Branson was mentored by Sir Freddie Laker, an aviation entrepreneur, who provided advice on the airline industry and encouraged Branson to enter the market with Virgin Atlantic.

Better Followers: Branson learned the value of bold thinking and seeking advice from experienced industry leaders, making him more open to diverse perspectives.

Passing It On: Branson mentors entrepreneurs through his various initiatives, including the Branson Centre of Entrepreneurship. He shares his experiences and encourages others to pursue innovative and disruptive business ideas.

Whose success could you contribute to as a mentor?

ACKNOWLEDGMENTS

I have to say a huge thank you to all the marvelous minds whose work has contributed to my own growth over the years and consequently ended up in this book in different forms.

SPECIAL THANKS!

I would like to say **THANK YOU** to some special people who really helped me with this book:

Angie Lightner

Lisa Hoffman

Joyce Lightner

Terri Lightner

ABOUT THE AUTHOR

"When you truly believe in yourself and what you are trying to accomplish, others will believe in you and your vision as well."

~ Mike T. Lightner

Mike Lightner is a retired Chief Master Sergeant from the United States Air Force with extensive knowledge and experience in team leadership and personnel development. In his last position, as the Aircrew Flight Equipment Career Field Manager, he oversaw the leadership, growth, development, and management of over 5,200 Total Force (Active Duty, Air National Guard, and Reserve Airmen, and civilian employees) worldwide. Additionally, Mike was responsible for the inspection, maintenance, acquisition, and sustainment of over $8 Billion in critical life sustaining aircrew and passenger safety, survival, and chemical defense equipment.

As a John C. Maxwell Certified International Coach, Teacher, and Speaker, Mike offers workshops, seminars, keynote speaking, and coaching,

THE UNTOUCHABLE WAY

designed to aid you in your personal and professional growth through study and practical application of proven leadership methods.

Mike's passion is to develop leaders who, in turn, have a passion to develop leaders. If this is the type culture you would like to create within your organization, he stands ready to help you achieve your goal!

mikelightner@d2dleadership.com

www.d2dleadership.com

OTHER BOOKS BY MIKE

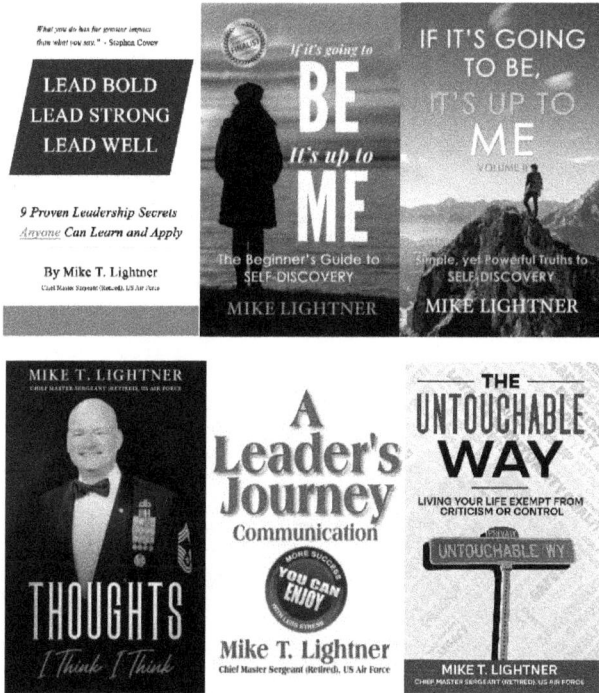

Available on Amazon